The
Rx-Express

Written By: Jaccie Hisashima and Shay Roth
Illustrated By: Shay Roth

To Pitt Pharmacy – thank you for your constant support throughout our wild endeavors.

Thank you for allowing us to share the profession of pharmacy over, under, and beyond the counter!

A Special Thank You to:
Dean Amy Seybert
Dr. Patricia Kroboth
Dr. Randy Smith
Dr. Ashley Yarabinec
Dr. Rhea Bowman
Dr. Thomas Nolin
All Pitt Pharmacy Faculty

You might think of a pharmacist as someone behind the counter.
But really they do so much more, more than you'd encounter!

PHARMACY

Join us as we bring our friend to
journey through the fields!
We'll visit our different pharmacist
friends to see what they can yield.
So all aboard our little van that's named Rx-Express,
We'll explore different paths that you can take that
surely will impress!

You're probably most familiar
with the pharmacists in the
community,
Working to keep their patients safe,
And to help boost their immunity!

Your immunity exists to keep you healthy and strong,
And pharmacists are here to help move it along!

Patients may also require more direct and intense care,
So we have pharmacists in hospitals, they are everywhere!

You vow to help patients big and small, ready to engage,
As a pharmacist you take an oath to care for each and
every age!

You can even find a pharmacist working in a lab,
Running some experiments, and answering
questions you may have!

You always want to make sure that a
medication will be successful,
You can use genetics to be more accurate
and careful!

Certain patients require unique formulations,
That pharmacists prepare, so they can take their medications!

Pharmacists help people
And many animals too,
So let's take a trip
And head to the zoo!

Even animals need care, for a
short or long duration,
And pharmacists can prepare
the medicine without hesitation!

To become a pharmacist you must go to class,
To learn about the body, and study hard to pass!

Here is Dr. Nolin, he is an expert in kidneys,
Improving patient outcomes, and keeping others
healthy!

You can counsel from your computer
through the internet online,
And help make a difference, anywhere,
anytime!

You can even work in your pajamas, from the comfort of your home.
But still be a professional, helping patients through the phone!

Safety is important, there is no doubt.
Data is collected, even after the study comes out!

Pharmacists can analyze the studies conducted,
To make sure they were appropriately and properly
constructed!

Now we'll take a look at the pharmaceutical industry,
Where drugs are designed with perfect symmetry.

Pharmacists play a role in this drug-making process,
Ensuring things go well for the company's progress!

Just like anything, pharmacy has its flaws.
So pharmacists work with the government to
help fix the laws.

Our voices are strong,
we all have influence
Go on, speak out, and
help make a difference!

Meet Dr. Kroboth, she's been through it all.
Questions about pharmacy? She's the one to call!

Now Dean Seybert helps her
students chase their dreams
By leading the school, with an
amazing team!

If she puts her mind to it
to work hard and study,
She knows without a doubt that
she can become anybody!

Now look in the mirror,
Go on, take a peek!
Look to the future,
All the dreams that you
seek.

When we look at you, we see with guarantee,
That you can chase your dream, and earn a
PharmD!

Meet the Authors
Jaccie Hisashima

Jaccie Hisashima is a current Doctor of Pharmacy Student in the University of Pittsburgh's School of Pharmacy Class of 2023. Jaccie was born and raised on the island of Maui, and knew her dream was to help people. Her favorite part about pharmacy is understanding the mechanisms of the drugs, and how they all interact with the body to help (or even cause discomfort) to a patient. Working in a psychiatric pharmacy actually heightened Jaccie's interest in psychiatric medications, so perhaps she will choose to pursue that further. Shay mentioned to Jaccie that she loved drawing, and thought why not make a Children's Book about pharmacy? As the Head Program Coordinator for PittPharmacy's PIER Program, her goal has always been to show her students the many paths you can take with a PharmD degree. This story allows younger children to read about the vast opportunities that exist for a pharmacist, and hopefully inspire them to learn more about this career.

Meet the Authors
Shay Roth

Shay Roth is a current Doctor of Pharmacy Student in the University of Pittsburgh's PharmD Class of 2024. Writing and illustrating a children's book has been a dream of hers for quite some time, and she is ecstatic to combine her passions for science and creativity to educate others on the various fields of pharmacy. Originally from Johnstown, Pennsylvania, Shay grew up visiting the city of Pittsburgh, and always wanted to pursue a career in the medical field following treatment at a children's hospital when she was young. Having worked in community, hospital, and clinic settings, Shay looks forward to continuing to explore the field of pharmacy as she prepares for her career. While Shay is unsure exactly where her career will take her, she is passionate about working with the underserved and providing the best possible care for all patients. When she is not studying, working, or drawing, Shay enjoys playing the piano and violin, hiking, and rescuing animals.